THE CHANTER'S TUNE

BoA.

THE
CHANTER'S TUNE

Valerie Gillies

Illustrations by Will Maclean

CANONGATE

First published in 1990
by Canongate Publishing Limited
17 Jeffrey Street, Edinburgh

© Valerie Gillies

British Library Cataloguing in Publication Data
Gillies, Valerie
The chanters tune
I. Title
821.914
ISBN 0-86241-286-2

Typeset by Speedspools, Edinburgh
Printed and bound in Denmark
by Norhaven Rotation

DEDICATION

for Liam

A child plays the chanter, thrills
To air on the reed, its vibrant tongue :
The oldest tune by the youngest one,
Sound-source, the birth of the world.

Acknowledgements

Acknowledgements are due to the editors of anthologies where a few of these poems appeared for the first time : *Natural Light* (Paul Harris Publishing/Waterfront, Edinburgh 1985); *New Writing Scotland 5* (Association for Scottish Literary Studies, 1987); *Voices of our Kind* (Chambers, 1989); *European Poetry in Scotland* (Edinburgh University Press, 1989).

'Rock Thrush Alone' was commissioned for *Leopardi: a Scottis Quair* (Edinburgh University Press, 1987).

Several of the poems were written for performance with the composer and virtuoso clarsach player Savourna Stevenson.

'The Ship of Women' was translated for Will Maclean, to accompany his box construction on that theme. The early sixteenth century original was first edited by W. J. Watson in *Scottish Verse from the Book of the Dean of Lismore* (Edinburgh 1937).

I am indebted to my husband for elucidating some of the difficulties of the Gaelic poems, and to Martin McLaughlin and Christopher Whyte for converting my Latin into Italian.

Contents

SEQUENCES

The Hawkshaw Head

A marble Roman head found at Hawkshaw, by Tweedsmuir.

(i)

He lies without moving inside the hill.
His eyes watch the clod above him:
tides of frost and summer fire split off his nose and ears.
The moor stretches its tarpaulin on a hoop bent round,
khaki camouflaging its soldier hidden underground.

The eyes and brow are a man's:
the folds in his face are from wearing sheetbronze,
the cheekpieces of a sports helmet, or one for war.
Torn from its niche, taken by Selgovae on a raid,
the head below the mouth is broken away.

The lips are one downward curve,
the combed locks of hair frame the severe face
carved in creamy crystalline marble.
Spherical, perfect as an egg, it's a wonderful head
to sculpt, or to steal for the power of the dead.

A trophy hanging by a saddle,
a severed head for companion at the feast,
an enemy's skull to speak out:
once, men carried it as loot into their own region
to instruct them in war, be talisman against the legions.

Then follows a mute millennium of burial
for the forehead furrowed like a browband,
for the unusually large eyes.
Until, turning earth not worked before, the cast-iron sock
of a plough strikes against what seems like rock.

The ploughscar fresh upon the crown
dents the skull in a newborn's fontanelle:
the head lifted out from the furrow
is larger than lifesize, a shock to the man at the ploughshare
when he is looked down by that imperious stare.

(ii)

Entertain us, magical head:
anyone coming towards you
finds you hospitable.
You persist, brain-stalk in marble,
after the death of your original.

Inform us, prophesy for us.
You could tell a tale or two:
you can move or speak
if we look long enough at you,
head, the soul's seat!

Tell us what to do
to avoid disaster,
tell us how to behave
to save ourselves from disillusion,
to forget both suffering and bravery.

Keep plague away
from your surrounding territory.
Come with us again
to where you were for a thousand years
and more, in Hawkshaw glen.

Once there, you can advise us
how to be free of history,
obliterate our human memory,
make us unaware of where we are
in our suicidal century.

(iii)

'I am no stranger to action,' says
the head, 'oh no, enough of history,
you are entering a new and exciting phase.

My Roman military mind can see
that the Lance tactical missile
might need to stay in your inventory.

For they'll go where they are told
while tough talking by commanders
won't make NATO's zero-zero option hold.

Fine, get rid of Cruise and Pershing,
but improve conventional forces,
make use of all their buttressing.

Use paratroops of the Airborne school
in operations, they remind me of when
I sent forward the cohorts from Gaul.

Be ready to implement your strategy
even in the superpowers' new detente
or you'll increase the risk I see.

You'll need negotiating skills
and diplomatic buzzwords too
for the hardliners, military and political.

If you don't have the ability
to meet the unknown attack
you'll add to your uncertainties.'

Many ways, a head can face:
is it thus the hawk
would be likely to speak his piece?

(iv)

Pax might be what he'd want to say
since he was one of their best brains :
if nations cancel nuclear weaponry,
the more time changes, the more it is the same.

Silence outweighs anything that's audible.
To be able to speak would make him less
than he is, and is, in fact, impossible.
The beauty of it is, his dumbness.

If he is somehow more than what he seems,
this ruined head, a broken stump of marble,
then it is up to me to show the *numen*
in awe of him, to salvage this one marvel.

I think it comes from lying long in one place
and one so rare, that he has his special
association and has acquired some grace.
Whatever there is, is almost visible.

The head shines with its own light, illuminates
our time with life-restoring vision.
Close your eyes, you can see straight
ahead his after-image in clearcut retention.

(v)

I came in with the curator
and laid my hand upon your head
but under these warm fingers
more marbledust was shed.
Who'll go first into oblivion
of us two?
One thing is certain,
it will not be you.
Trying to see whether your nose was chipped
off by frost or foe
I felt blood in my own nostril
gather and flow
but could not stop it:
in the museum gallery
it fell crimson on my present
of white silk from Italy,
where other visitors could see it
on my hand and scarf.
Red on white, beside your skull,
I bleed, alive, your epitaph.
You give me beauty
though I can give nothing, and in no eternity
can I hope to see
you, or you the shade of me.

(vi)

CAPUT
Wise head
on no shoulders,
onion-bulb, corn-ear,
ash-bud, spear-blade,
bolt-head, gate-timber,
poppy-capsule, dandelion-clock,
drum's membrane, column's capital,
coin's impression, river-source,
lingam's potency, capstone,
headland, plough-iron,
yeast-froth, ale's foam-top :
each thing that has a head
rises towards time's surface.
Distinguish the portrait head, well wrought,
and in it so many kilos of marble,
concentrate on the realistic human face :
eye to eye, your discourse is
without the whole body
a deliberate honouring
by head alone.
CAPUT
Carve the head
as the main means
of identifying the man.
To cap it all, Cuchulainn has arrived
with heads fastened on his chariot,
he shakes them at his enemies.
Conall Cernach has boasted
he sleeps with a head under his knee
and when such a warrior sits crosslegged
he rests one hand on a severed skull.

Livy tells how the Boii tribe
cut off the Roman general's head,
clean it out and gild it
and use it as a cult vessel.
Then, the Celts say that Bran's head
remains alive after the death of his body,
it can sing and entertain,
it presides over the otherworld feast.
Sweeney meets three talking heads on the road,
they yell and give chase to him,
they frighten him into a fit of flying.
And so, you hard-face, you survivor,
whether displayed in a skull-niche in some temple
or, nowadays, impaled on the rod in the museum,
be cherished above all our other treasures,
regenerate this world,
shape our course,
Hawkshaw
Head.

(vii)

Across the moor, there was another ploughman
who turned up gold armlets in a cist,
but it's not that kind of treasure, this,
that through the earth's substratum
grows prominent and moves
like a shoot toward the surface,
the head rising from the furrow-groove
till, above ground, he shows his face.

He has got his knowledge of the world already
and from the high end of the valley
two ravens fly near
to speak into his ears.

The Ship of Women

From the Gaelic of The Bard MacIntyre
for Will MacLean

(i)

What's the ship that's on Loch Inch,
Have we had any report since?
What is it the open loch reveals
And the land no longer conceals?

That's what I'd like to ask, at the launch
Who let loose the galley on the loch?
Though it is early morning here,
The loch is full of anger.

Was it a rough wind from the top of a ben
Or bitter storms from a streaming glen
Which expelled the hulk from the beachhead
Out onto the rough dangerous roadstead?

You, young man who saw the ship go
On the fearsome tossing tideflow,
What's so marvellous about her,
Can you tell the makeup of her timber?

An old crate, without rudder, without oak,
We have not seen her like afloat;
She's a ship completely made of leather,
She's not seaworthy in any weather.

Boards of the wings of black beetles
From her prow along her gunwales:
Headless rivets join her skin
On the high chill ocean.

What's the crew in the black ship
Drawing her along the wave's lip?
A company without fellowship or sense:
Women! with their whims intense.

A band garrulous and loud,
A negligent and vapid crowd,
Captious, greedy flibbertigibbets,
Evil desires while chanting ditties.

A bad stock, wordy over ale,
Going in gangs matchmaking they sail
Where each can pass the microphone along,
Confused and drunk and full of song.

That party whose fiery fannies singe
Go up and down the two sides of Loch Inch.
They have all been thrown amiss
Onto the cold ridge of the abyss.

No good woman ventures on board,
She won't be satirized on that accord :
The worst of women tend to be
With nobody helping them on the sea.

Chase that ship away out of the loch
Onto the tidal brine, mobile and rough.
Let there be a wind to hustle her on
As far as the old stream of Shannon.

Let us leave the evil leaky hulk
On stormy stream, not watertight or caulked,
And its cargo of noxious women consigned
Without psalm or sea-creed to the brine.

(ii)

A ship has come out onto Loch Rannoch,
The hostile, spiteful old crock,
A ship that's roving, light and prompt
With toothy set of oars and broadbeamed rump.

That ship of which we speak in rhyme
No craftsman shaped before this time,
And so it's right to tell her wonders,
To rate her timbers in their numbers.

Boards made of bramble-leaves
Bud from her sides' extremities.
Briar nails in planks no oakum sealed,
Her rivets bristle along her keel.

Strings of withered rushes dry on
Thwarts of smooth-faced docken;
Her oars are sprigs of russet bracken:
Cope with cold sea-hate, they can!

A mast of stiff reeds trimmed
Against a sea surly and grim,
Behind the mast, a rotting yard:
Likewise the crew on deck are marred.

With cables made of barley husks
She sails upon the waters' rush;
Aloft, a fluttering sail, hoist
While currents make a bitter haste.

'Ship of she-devils' is what everyone calls
The ship of strange shape, her form unusual.
There ought to be more crew inside
To row her up against the tide.

The women, drunk and haughty,
Hold in her stern a converse naughty,
The salt sea comes over their thighs :
Without good luck, their fate is realised.

Naked shameful women do not scorn
To lie on a harsh bed of thorns.
The bilgewater over their feet in the hulk,
A blast of wind blows off their babbling talk.

On each side of her the women gabble,
Standing up on the deck of the vessel
Or crouching where billows don't deter
A ranting, flyting wind of words.

Those common vulgar women raise themselves
On that mast elevated above everybody else,
Their rumps exposed to the wind's arts,
A wisp of fire around those parts.

These women, insolent and proud,
Are on their ship's topmast and shrouds.
Ahead lies neither reef nor rock,
Only the open sea kindling its wrath.

Thunderstorm out on the great seaways,
The firmament of the air enraged,
Madness on the stony skerries there,
The current of the sea hides her.

Rough showers on a March wind, sharp
Bare rocks surround the swift bark,
Mobbed by the waves in furious surge,
The wind hustles around in its urge.

Stormblast with wind sleety and snowy
Screws the waves up against the company :
She's no safe craft against a rough sea,
She's a dirty ship and holds them lightly.

For all the wickedness they have done,
Vengeance is exacted from the evil ones :
Drubbed from head to foot, that's it,
Storm-stayed out on the sea's tit.

A devil's cargo in the ship of Colin's son,
Lucifer's women for round-eyed Duncan,
With their habits and contagious charms,
Their warpaint on, women with dyed palms.

The Mugdrum Sequence
for Derek Robertson

(i)
River Island

from Dante's *Purgatorio*, Canto 1, lines 100–105

Questa isoletta intorno ad imo ad imo,
là giù colà dove la batte l'onda,
porta dei giunchi sovra il molle limo:
null'altra pianta che facesse fronda
o indurasse, vi puote aver vita,
però che a le percosse non seconda.

All around this little island in its reaches low
    down there where the wave is beating,
    tall reeds from soft mud can grow:
no other plant can live there, bearing
    leaves or hardening in its prime,
    that will not bend when tides are battering.

(ii)
The Death of Adonis

Three go through the world,
boar, hound and man.
Blood anemones
redden the slopes after rain.

(iii)

Reed Harvest

Pancake flat, plank of gold,
little tuft, reeds and rushes,
channel changer, moving shallows,
the islandman, a life fisher,
the island goddess sways the flood.

Solid stone, fluid river,
yellow eyot within the firth,
by stone pillar and low hill
an islet stands, a small world,
a dry site at sea level.

A brazen boar, a ridgeback,
beast of the chase, wood sense,
in mudbank the boat of oak,
a dugout canoe, boar openmouthed,
the eyeboat is preserved in mud.

Duckshooter trapped waderheight,
gunfire repeats at twilight tide,
shouts and cries on true bank,
a boar swims to the island,
a tusky one to Mugdrum.

(iv)

After Mugdrum

View now and see
the Mugdrum stone :
when this is gone,
so shall we be.

Get us an amulet,
a horn to form one piece with the helmet.
The most effective for us to survive
is a tusk taken while the boar is alive,
the boar who was a king,
Silver Bristle : like silver wings
those glittering bristles show the path
he takes through the forest in his wrath.

Carve his intricacy
thereon,
if it be gone,
then so shall we.

In the greatest wind in the world
a smoke is blowing south, unfurled
and not being turned, you understand,
by the skies or over land.
That is the fire on shore
where a huntsman singes a wild boar.

On the stone hunt frieze
horsemen and boars together
are too far weathered
for certainty.

Where they left a message for us
we cannot read without the tusk :
how that hunting-party ended,
what hound a chieftain's life defended
as through them all one boar rushed free,
swam the Tay and out to sea.
The stone stands to mark a terminal :
last seen here, the oldest animal.

(v)

The Mugdrum Strathspey

Carpow and Mugdrum,
Gillies Burn, Mugdrum,
Wester Clunie, Mugdrum,
Skirlbear, Mugdrum.

Abernethy, Mugdrumn,
Sweerie, Mugdrum,
Lumbennie,Mugdrum,
Whinnybank, Mugdrum.

Butter Well, Mugdrum,
Pow of Lindores, Mugdrum,
Clatchard Craig, Mugdrum
Denmylne, Mugdrum.
Tay and Earn, Mugdrum,
Tay and Earn, Mugdrum.

The fighting men of Carpow ground,
    a horseman caught in mud,
the baited boar with foamy tusk,
    fishers swept away by flood,
they seek the shifting Wonder Bank
    where snouts of water tug.

The curved tusk at the new moon
    meets swordblade on The Hard,
his little eye sees all the ways
    but the Kerewhip Bank's a star:
the man who wears the sheet-bronze scales
    has skin without a scar.

LYRICS

Spelt Wheat

Two lips swell,
grain of truth expel.
The dark split
fertile slit
the open maw
shapely flaw
the ripe gape
seems opaque,
the mouth-welt
sends up spelt.
It germinates
movement's rate.

Bearded wheat,
selective breed,
responds to light,
grows man-height,
seeds on field
the risen yield.
The acres' sheet
makes wheat
the summer stain
so explain
its show,
field yellow.

Grains in the round
are ground,
ears pressed
into flesh,
burst to be grown
blood and bone.
They'll have got
mouths stopped
with wheat
who speak.

Rapper Song

I'm not just a pretty word you know
Baking my rough bread in the winter stove.
I can make out in the distance animals of light,
Hold conversation with the mountains by night,
Have words with the waterhorse, or speak
To pure things like the folded peaks.

Wearing frost bells on the backs of my hands
I gesture and step the thinking dance.
With an ivory whistle for my voice disguiser
My song will make you none the wiser.
Iron tongues with buzzing beads to hum
Rub spirit music on a talking drum;
Slit and strung nutshells on a rope
Make trappings for my harnessed antelope.

I rear green thistles beside dewy roads,
Small stars and young shoots in stackyards.
A stick for panther by the door is pinned,
My roof was whirled away by winds.
Stones and tributes enter my dream:
They come through the window where I lean.

To a Butterfly in an Overgrown Garden

This butterfly to the flowerhead clings,
forming a new and fairer flower of wings.

You give up your own identity :
now, are you flower or butterfly ?

It's in the nature of the pretty
to survive by mimicry.

I look down on you from above :
who gave the self away for love ?

You look up at me from below
and use your wings to go.

If I see you in terms of me,
refresh me with your ambiguity.

Miles, Born at Midwinter

You take your chance
  When winter breaks bright,
You choose the dance
  Rather than flight.

Your first step on the floor
  Is going to dance like air,
A new smile at the door
  Is handsome and fair.

You change darkness and lead
  To gold when you will,
Sonorous and mobile your tread ;
  Yet you can stay still.

Welcome Miles, you already know
  Who you now are :
Be a man of light, and show
  The sun is a strong star.

Fruid Water

Tune : 'Logan Water'

Fruid Water, furthest of all from the sea,
yours is the voice that means far more to me
than the salty wave flowing up the beach
of a great stretch of ocean I may never reach.
Little I care for foaming breakers on the shore
or the surface calm that moves so much slower
if I hear your notes that are sweeter than the surf
of all the different waters of the earth.

I don't need to see the whale or sea-wrack,
the flight of the gannet, the diving of the shag,
I long to watch your trout or your owl flying low,
on your banks I hear the sudden hooves of the roe.
Each of us finds that you can quench our thirst,
stream and surrounding terrain belong together from the first.
In the face of the light you become, through your quality,
like an eye reflecting us in transparency.

Huge masses of water roll in the oceans,
deep currents circulate, of gigantic proportions,
but where you flow freely and trickle over stones
you play with waves in rhythm, vibrate and sing alone.
Out of vapour you have come back to liquid,
you return in your course every time to Fruid.
Evaporating, loop with air currents and precipitate :
between earth and heaven you mediate.

Your moving form issuing from the hills
twists in strands of water changed like turning veils ;
they make a rope that spirals down the glen,
new water falling through it to refresh men.
I can tell by the current as it swirls along
where it comes from, what rocks cause its tension,
and I praise your wave shapes through which the water flows,
for they remain the same, and rarely go.

Cardrona Woods

The Tweed drawn downhill
in following the seaward pull
swings from side to side.
Faster in rhythm
it winds to and fro
where the valley narrows
at the blackthorn fort.

Water is always on its way
somewhere, on this summer's day
its greatest stream transpires upward;
gallons drawn through woodland
pass into the atmosphere,
circulate over the whole earth
from this blackthorn fort.

Sap streams in the pines,
goes up to interplay with air:
earth, trees and sky
make up one totality.
Water flows in living veins,
trees spread vascular systems
through the fort of the blackthorn.

Vitalised by each fresh wave
all this life is really water,
whether river or wood's vapour,
deer, trout or men enclose
the currents of their stream
moving to fluid laws
around Cardrona fort.

The Rock of Hawthornden

Tune : 'The Winter It is Past'

At the rock of Hawthornden,
steep outcrop well-loved by men
since the day they first fortified its crag,
put a hand to the rockface,
it is magnetized in place
by the fiery core of the old magma.

Marked with clefts and caves,
ferns and trees within its waves,
sewn with deadwood petrified in seams,
crystals and glittering stones embed
shining eyes upon this head
while through its ivy wreath there darts a wren.

In India such rocks
worshipped like beasts or gods
are visited by pilgrims walking on the plain ;
only here in Scotland
it takes a solitary stand
among discords of chainsaw and firing range.

River Esk so far below
turns sunwise in its flow
round the rock and the house on its rampart,
where wooded shades sun never clears
keep dark four hundred years
since the man of Hawthornden lived at its heart.

His was a white melancholy
suspended on this promontory
washed by weathers high above the wooded valley,
a house rich in angled shapes,
turrets and crow-step gables :
for the art of thinking he rebuilt his sanctuary.

Now Drummond of Hawthornden
once wrote to his true friend,
'Where I love, there I love for years'
and from this place he loved
his spirit cannot now remove;
he is at last his own rockform here.

Harp Music

from the Gaelic of Sileas na Ceapaich

Welcome back, clarsach,
    Since I put you away firmly;
Now if I could keep you in
    You wouldn't go out in a hurry.

Melodious the ribbed tidebank of strings
    Being tuned up so near;
I am overjoyed by your yellow sweet body
    Played close by my ear.

If I were a rich heiress
    You would always be around to sing;
I would hear you make love to me
    After waking in the morning.

Dearer than fiddle or bass,
    Organ or any instrument, I'm sure,
My choice beyond all other music
    Your strings sounding through firm hard boards.

Young Harper

Above Tweed Green levels
Maeve first raises the harp.

Prosper her hand that plucks
then clenches fist like a jockey.

Grip inside thighs
the colt with a cropped mane.

Turn blades on the curved neck
bristling with spigots.

Out from the rosewood forest
came this foal of strung nerve.

Stand in your grainy coat,
let her lift elbows over you.

Keep her thumbs bent
and fingers hard to do the playing.

Eight summers made them, clarsach,
I freely give you my elder daughter.

Fresco Girl

for Louise Johnstone

A girl raises her foot to step
Off onto the dancing-floor.
Profane and sacred time have met
Here on its beaten shore.
She is as she is today.

Others danced in the first place,
Now she does likewise,
Emerging on the threshold of space,
With hollow palms she claps her thighs.
She casts off naturally

From this moment, and away
She goes back in youth and vigour
To see and sing the waking
Dream, a sleep-dancing figure.
She hears the lyre play.

If a territory can be lost
Her trance prevents it.
If a life can be botched
Her turns avoid that.
Chant the old charm, a way

To share the dance-ground with the goddess
For some of the time. Her cap's on,
And the broad folds of her dress
Overfall clean limbs flowing along.
She begins us again every day.

Trio

You're asking me
About the cult of the three,
Well, let's see:

Threefold goddess, a trio of ivory girls,
Three hills, linked triple whorls like triskels.
Three times three, is the moon in eclipse

When she shows another hue beneath her silver
and bronze instruments clash in vain to help her.
The hinds feed upon trefoil in high pasture.

The ram-bearer sounds a beast-muzzle trumpet.
A maiden with a white dagger is youngest of the triad,
She looks joyful as you approach, as you leave she's sad.

She daubs her face with gypsum, whiteness
Of white clay in honour of the grain-goddess
Who clears your sight as you read this.

Her dancers spring and bound, three bent legs
Draw a spiral with nine turns, three whirligigs.
Europe's vertiginous history widens and grows giddy.

Girls on a Swing

The girls are swinging
together on the plastic seat
in the mid-light evening.

The arbour is made of pleated peach
twinned trees, on these
one bird is perched for each.

The girls' swinging so light
is the rising and setting of the moon,
its semi-circular flight.

They hold ropes of orange yarn:
their young faces
turn on the wind's charm.

Wherever they fly,
wherever they look, they fructify
the garden, fruit trees and the sky.

Eagle Man

for Hugh MacDiarmid

His is the face of a sea-eagle,
The eyes looking into light.

The molten circle of his face turns,
Panning like a radar dish.

As hawk god or eagle man
He dances the creation dance.

The first time he flies
He raises the disc of the sun,

He carries a feather of light
Away from the shadow edge :

Sharp head, solar eagle,
Stars shrink to zero.

William Johnstone, Farmer and Artist

'As I go to my studio I hear my father saying, sadly, "Ah,
Johnstone, think what a great farmer you might have been!"'
Last words of his autobiography, *Points in Time*.

His eye travels over
the line of the Pictland bull
and makes out the mass and weight
by his sense of design and space:
the same eye singles out
Bardolph, perfect in his conformation,
to stand at Satchells farm.

His mind moves around
cult animals and wonder beasts
and opens out their form
to his students of the abstract:
the same mind has found
the sheep under the snow
lying like the spokes of a wheel
beneath the rolling rhythm
of the visual field.

The hand that ploughs the first furrow
loads his brush and continues a line:
the furrows become a pattern,
the ground changes colour,
team and man are one with the field.
The earth artist, how he sees things,
lends his meaning to their meaning.

Youth in a Beret

It was in the museum, about halfway,
I was fixed to the spot by the look
From the head of a youth in a beret
Carved in wood like a grainy root.

Once a Renaissance master
Made chips fly with the adze,
With chisel-blade whittled faster
A youth to make hearts glad.

And today when I left him
To go out of the revolving doors,
Here I saw one and the same
Youth in a beret, gold in his ears.

Each pushed a spoke of the wheel
Where time's door rotates its spin.
Not one meets the other revealed,
But in Hades I'd recognise him.

Young Farmer at the Cashmere Goat Sales

He's clean of limb, and his newshaven chin rests on his hands
That fold over the long crook at throat-height. He stands
In his turned-up hillboots, bestrides this slippery deck,
Colossus in tweeds, with a camera and a thousand-pound cheque.
He moves the crook to stir the beasts about some,
Telling by their big knees if there's more growth to come.

He tries their coats between forefinger and thumb,
The long white topfleeces like a spiral perm.
He feels for the dense handful of cashmere beneath,
Combs the riches per ounce these male kids will bequeath.
A young girl hangs over the corner-rail to hear his jargon:
He reaches a finger to her hair, to gauge the first carding.

Landface

A craggy northeast face,
a woman in her place
on the station platform at Montrose:
a leather coat and red stilettos,
tawny curls, scarlet shirt,
brown legs, silver anklet.
Sitting waiting while crowds are on the run
she's at ease in the wind and the sun.
Hard the features of her race,
handsome stays the country face:
she takes a train for Aberdeen
through fields her folk have seen.
The seasons come back round again,
where they were, they'll be the same,
the wind in its great power whirls
a northwoman in its circles.

Tay Bridge, Night

Our train and passengers spin at a height
above sea level, it bottles us
up at the launch of the night.
We grow momentous.
Across ravelling space
piers and girders link,
eyes shine outside, a face
on the blink.

Skeletons make no fuss
when they join arms with us.
If we look vain
they lead us in the train
of their steelbone embrace.
Combining at this point in space,
strange couplings, these:
youth and joy, fear and disease.
We who are full
of life will fall.
The bony ones arrest
us, clasped to their gridiron chests,
as to the unexpected mate
we feel the pull and gravitate.

Berserk in Morningside

They caught the young madwoman
And wouldn't let her go
In the cold light of the afternoon.

Gripped by the wrists, she soon
Ceased struggling and whispered, 'No!'
In the cold light of the afternoon.

Her breast floated like a half-moon
Where she twisted to one side, so
They caught the young madwoman

And around the naked human
Others, fully clothed, concealed her show
In the cold light of the afternoon.

Her whiteness had illumined
The street till her overthrow;
They caught the young madwoman
In the cold light of the afternoon.

Hunter's Mask

He lived alone, up country,
further than the eucalyptus slopes,
higher than one day's coffee blossom.

His verandah perched above
all the southern highland valleys,
the rent and chasm of them.

He wouldn't talk much
or come along with us.
He turned and he looked away.

He lent me
a beautiful gun in its case,
two interlocking pieces.

Loading at a tankbund,
I fitted barrel and stock together;
they were well-oiled, gleaming.

Others told me, years before,
he was on foot in the forest
and when he turned round

a bear gripped him by the head.
In the bite of claws and teeth
he kept to one purpose.

He pressed close in its embrace
until his free hand
found his revolver and fired.

Then the bear rampant
fell back, taking
half his face with it.

I saw duck fly, moon rise,
the scrape of the road on the hill.
I cleaned his gun carefully.

'He never lends it out,'
they said. Being young,
they made me scared to return it.

Going back up to the house,
I thought of that bear-hug.
I regarded his one lunar eye:

the clawmarked bear path,
the wide goggle and strap
on the helmet of his skull,

the frightened and the frightening.
His courage continued
its halfmoon shine, the hunter's mask.

Infertility Patient

'I could never have enough children.' Katherine Mansfield.

To lift another woman's child
is like carrying a bundle of barbed wire.
And one who will let himself be held
stirs every bereaved desire.

Between collarbone and breast
his hard head makes an impression :
a dent in a white quilt
someone's secretly been sleeping on.

My hands fall empty in my lap
when she lifts him away.
I can share, as I give him up,
only his backwards look with no wave.

She's the fertile one while I am not.
Inject a dye and see my tubes are drawn
blocked and scarred, death's first print I've got
in me : you month, rat's jaw, I see you yawn.

Cigarette in the Bath

'Nobody said –
and nothing I'd read
told me what it was going to be like.
He looked so small last night
and ugly, but what with the epidural I had
the birth was not too bad.
The worst is now, I've got scared –
they've taken him into intensive care.
He's scrunched up tight, with lifesavers,
all wired up in the incubator.
     I want to walk out, it's not fair –
I mean, he could stay there
and I could just go
off, if I want to, on my own.
There are different things, they say,
wrong with him, anyway.
But when I see him try –
he really tries
to draw the bliss of breath.
So I stay, I can't forget.'

What She Told Her Friend

*A variation on the classic Tamil love poem by Venmanipputi, a
woman poet of the first century A.D.*

At a late-night party watched by no-one
who had not been drinking,
in sofas like groves
filled with leaves and birdsong,
on the banks of chintz
clustered with flowers,

                                    I sat in his lap
                                    my arm around his neck.

My eyes could not see him

                                    it was too smoky
                                    and he got too close

my ears could not hear him

                                    full of his kisses
                                    and snaps of laughter.

But my hand grew beautiful
on his shoulder
and shrivelled to bone
when I took it away.

                                    What am I to make of this?

Quair Water

A Scots quair, ripples in a ream
flicker the length of stream,

a quire deckle-edged enough
to turn words in the water I quaff.

I have a say, learn the way
of stories from Dalgleish and Grey,

farmer and gamekeeper. They know
what's underneath the skim of snow

we call the present. They can tell
where the grin-stanes went from the mill,

which shepherd found old bottles by the burn
at the whisky-still, and frequently returns.

And which are the trout with whiskers on,
gold as saffron, and where they've gone:

the ones they called the Bessie-Beardies,
they tried to catch with snare-wire, as laddies.

Why do the men who used to plough
blacken fields with nitrates, and leave now?

The seepage, the wash comes flooding down
and clear Quair is discoloured and drowned.

Saint Bryde's Well, that healing spring
is covered with flagstones, but still running.

No natural balance left, it's up to man
to match that flow of purity, and plan.

Shepherd's Calendar

It was after Chernobyl we heard of it,
that they slaughtered all the Lapps' reindeer,
buried a radioactive hundred thousand in a great pit.

While up the Quair Water our lambs were born
with one eye in the middle of their heads,
with no tails or no back passage or weird horns.

It was the same for Greeks after Oedipus,
everything shows the signs of a miasma,
a time when the wrong people are ruling us.

Stobo

The Stobo bus has just passed by.
Two whole hours before another comes,
So what's to be done?

The path runs, creates its way
In the sunlight, quickens my steps
Walking, the simple best.

Stobo, glen of staves,
Whose hills are the wave-stop
When floods bear off the crop,

Is flush with stillness.
The eternal present breathes a sigh
Where the Stobo bus has just passed by.

Tweed's Well

for Tim Neat

The high moor is an open palm
of a hand, lined with rivulets.
On a winter's morning, warmed with walking,
we cross marsh and rough pasture.
First, we meet two roebuck, shining tines.
Then in our path stand two pony stallions,
shaggy, mop-maned, hooves' whirligigs of hair.

The well rises in a little mound, flanked
by two blackface rams with curling horns,
upraised heads, deepset eyes, noses' broad wedge.
They watch, and they let us approach
in a straight line, not looking to either side.
The child, the first to find the well,
moves sunways round about the place.

Stoop for a palm of water, among green cresses,
drink a sip of knowledge, it runs clear,
a headwater emerging from its wreath of moss.
Riversource for roebuck and stallion and ram,
a spring from another world, beneficial and pure,
joins the cold streams near the watershed.
Stand up to return, the animals nuzzle and lick us.

At Athelstaneford

Athelstaneford is a rich ground, eagerly held
since people first searched it out and settled
long ago on the crest of the crag's height.
Fortified, they gripped grain and bronze tight
and drew a rib pattern like the tide
of strip agriculture on the slope side.

This year new cottagers built a round room
in the open valley below the hilltop fort, and soon
their windows and doors stand wide
to admit friends walking side by side.
Lines of cabbages and onions ranked by hoe will
copy the ideal strips high on the hill.

An automatic scarecrow with its hooter
frees the broad field of intruders;
speeding cars shave the lanes of their share
of summer grass and hold the road bare,
while townee guests with glass in hand
fall over in the grass when they try to stand.

Ernespie House, near Castle Douglas

The children are returning to the country of an ancestor,
That young girl disinherited when she eloped with her lover.
Wandering beside the long house and well-built stables,
They cross broad lawns, past urns and white summer tables
To the stately trees and rides beyond the slabbed stone steps
Of a grass-grown walled garden, where traces of old paths are left.
House now hotel, in your wood-lined room there is a cocktail bar
And in your dancing-hall sound discos, loud, ill-starred.
The stripling children go running up and down the steps so often
To spy, above the field of corn, the heads of the standing stones,
And within another ring, beneath the ancient tree, the rim
Of Oscar's grave, inscribed 'Faithful hound. Remember him.'

Hound of the noble folk of Ernespie,
Hound of the adept accurate McGhie!
These woods and lands were the gift of the Bruce
For killing a raven with a spear's single cast
And for fighting to win at Bannockburn.
It makes a good story, whatever else of the past we learn.

Where are your sons so active and keen of eye,
The horses and the deerhounds, where are they?
Where is that girl tall and lovely in her grace
And the people who once lived in this place?
Ernespie, record that today saw home a lost son,
Walking the forfeit estate to find his fortune is bygone,
While near stable and stall the hot sun will perpetuate
Only the shadow of a girl who leans her arm along the gate.

The Net Sinker

White boat, do not leave me alone
at the edge of the ocean.

My tall yellowhaired helmsman
leant out, leant out
leant out over the water
and let fall the weighted cask.

He buried my loveletters to him
under seething waves, under seething waves
under waves where no-one could read them
or see my photograph alongside seatrout.

The sound of water at his boat's foot
where he knew, where he knew
where he knew the strait to be very deep
he dropped it and the sea accepted it.

The stone star's fall through the curving waves
words of mine, words of mine
written words of mine like net sinkers
fell to the depths of his mind.

Since then, the rain's hissing or the sea's mumbling
my first singing, my first singing
hear my first singing and take your boat out
to where the waves kiss and kiss again.

In the south-east I walk out in the storm
let it drift, let it drift
let your heart drift over its diaphragm of sand
and turn still warm to me.

White boat, do not leave me alone.

The Mermaid's Song

Few men hear the mermaid's song,
Fewer get a right view of one.
A wave hitting then withdrawing with its roar
Reveals a girl balanced between rocks and shore:
An outward-facing head, with ears or gills,
Her little mouth half-open like a shell's,
A thin ridge running down the centre of the nose
From which raised rims sweep back along the jaws.
Her body is moulded at the midriff
And, slightly hipped, goes woman into fish.

Braiding her hair in a four-cord plait
She holds up her right hand to push it back
And her paw from the knuckle to the wrist
Is covered in gold, rich scales upon her fist.
Cut on the slant, her seagreen eyes
Are shaped elliptical and incised,
Watching the course of a ship under sail
She dives and tosses up her finny tail.
To see her hold her infant in her arm,
Suckling her young, forebodes the coming storm.

Her torso with its every twist
Changes life's music, it insists
Her sighs be wrung in rhyming series
Of little sounds recovered from the seas,
With voice of wave and wind sealong
The flow of sorrow drowns in her song.
Her throat and breast wear brightness
That her lyric power suggests,
A fabulous beast upon a stone who lay
Singing once or twice within an island bay.

Cloud and Shadow, Corsica
for Jonathan Robertson

The winds approach their rocky island,
Turn up a cloud, and start a wing,
Shadow the sea that waits to land :
Live air signs plus to everything.

The Old Woman's Reel

She is at the small deep window
looking through and out:
the Aran islands, rock and seawater,
lie all about.
A face strong in poverty's hauteur
is hers, then and now.

Being a young woman in Flaherty's film
'Man of Aran',
she nearly drowned in the undertow
by the boat where she ran.
He kept on filming even though
he thought her dead on the rockrim.

A body plaited by water twine
they carried ashore:
partnered in the ocean's set dance
by two men or more.
The sea had had its chance
to peel her off by the shoreline.

Now in her great old age
toothless and tough,
the island music still delights her:
one dance is not enough.
The tunes of a people poor and cut off there
have a special power to engage.

Drawn upright, her stiff bones
already dancing,
she spins, not on one foot
but on her stick, tap-balancing.
While to one side like a pliant offshoot
a little girl mimics her, unbeknown.

The Brocken Spectre

On the May morning I flew to Orkney
I thought the loveliest thing in the sky today
Would be your head, my darling man,
Where it travels everywhere within mine.

When I overtook the wind and the birds in flight
I kept the thought of you with me as the very type
Of male beauty, your shapely skull and weatherbeaten skin,
While the plane bucked north into a strong headwind.

With my back to the sun and out of the blue
Supported within heaped cloud, I flew
Where I saw through the window, in mid-air reflection
Gliding and straying over cloud, a strange apparition.

Some metres off, the rising sun gave me the spectral sight
Of a circle displaying colours by refractive light :
At the nucleus of brilliant hues in a series of bands
Was the image of a head, emanation of an aerial man.

It floated alongside me, the whole spectrum in the ring.
I flew on : the spectre did the same.
Was something visible in the play of colour, or nothing but
The way in which light rays are broken up ?

That it was my own thought, is the simple explanation,
Haunted by a handsome man in rainbow precipitation
Through air and water, mediating elements
Whose laws impress themselves upon my sense.

My illusory hope, to reach that airy sphere
From which you derive your features here:
When I looked for you and saw you in that light
You gave such radiance that angels couldn't be more
bright.

Your painted head, full of chromatic possibilities,
Is where colours can discover themselves perfectly.
It's true, your form might go out into the spaces of the air
Across the gap between me and your spectre there.

What does the pilot think, used to seeing a halo above
ground?
Or do I follow my delusion alone, my darling, in the
round?
Like the small plane and its luminous target-mark
We think we are separate, but we are not.

Lullaby on a Country Bus

Mairi's face on fields reflected,
white one in this girlhood bed
lays sleeping on a country bus
her red-gilt head.

Harp hills, high shapes
outside float by,
over part-ploughed fields her face
seems to fly.

Talking breath distils
above her barleycorn hair
to water on the windows,
my morning-fair.

Were you with Mairi Mhor in Glen Ose?
Do ballads sing you between two rivers?
With Silis composing at Beldornie
or with Marie at Craigmillar?

All of them in your Scottish face,
little smudge of gold and silver,
Is the child a sea, or a drop
of fresh water?

Sleeping heads on open fields:
you may well ask me
how far the beauty
is meant to be.

Notes:
Mairi Mhor nan Oran – Big Mary of the Songs: 19th century poet of
  the Clearances.
Silis na Keppoch – Gaelic poet.
Marie at Craigmillar – Mary Queen of Scots.

My Friend's Smiling Face

When I look at him,
at my friend's face,
how distant he is from me
I'm told by electricity.

It's the incidence of light,
these evanescent potentials
that my retina absorbs
in a continuous crowd of throbs.

The rhythmic shifting points
for the spongework of the brain
stream into my optic cup
and a little picture is set up.

My friend's smiling face,
tiny, two-dimensional
and outside me, now surrounds
me as the storm showers around.

Electrical leaks conjure him
for me, show him upside-down:
a portrait the eyeball paints
on nerve fibres to my brains.

He's thrown upright here
and I move forward till
how close he is to see
other senses tell me.

The Ericstane Brooch

The gold cross-bow brooch,
The Emperors' gift to an officer,
Was lost on the upland moor.
The pierced work and the inscription
Lay far from human habitation.

It worked on time and space
And they were at work on it.
What could withstand them?
But it was waiting for the human,
To address itself to a man or woman.

In the wilderness it meant nothing.
The great spaces dissolved its image,
Time obliterated its meaning.
Without being brought in,
It was less than the simplest safety-pin.

Now the brooch is transporting the past
To the present, the far to the near.
Between the two, its maker and wearer
And watcher live mysteriously.
Who is this who values it so seriously?

It exists, it has been seen by him.
If it speaks, it can only say
'He lost me.' And we reply, 'Who?
For he can also be our loss,
This moment floating face-down in the moss.'

Dumb replica: the original is in Los Angeles.
How is it, the man once destroyed,
His brooch continues boundlessly?
Our very existence is what it defies:
We no longer see what once we scrutinized.

The Sandman

Do not fear,
my little sweeting,
the atmosphere's
uneven heating,
for Sandman's here.

If you close
your eyes at night
you will not lose
the awful light,
now Sandman's here.

When you wake
to see a day
that throws and shapes
and fires the clay,
then Sandman's here.

Never ask
who breathes a sigh,
with radiant dust
he'll touch your eyes,
a Sandman's here.

Now a blight
has overrun
the fairest satellite
of the sun,
the Sandman's here.

Hush my baby
sleepy-eyes,
Chaos, our lady,
comes to your cries,
and Sandman's here.

The Wish Charm

Go to the hill with greyhounds,
Lurchers and longdogs along with you
Which are both clever and swift
To follow their quarry by sight.

Weave them round you like snakes
And you will never bend the head.
I see no sickbeds for you,
Light of foot on the hill.

The Man in the Moss

There is one marsh nobody reclaims.
Over rusty water, the reedbeds
Trail ochre strips and shreds.
From time to time, a straw will stir
As if someone draws air
Through it, down below the surface again.

Turf banks are riddled by watervoles.
As a girl, I ran along the margin lightly,
Chasing a rabbit between me and the collie.
It shot in below the bank and hid there.
I lay my length, fingertip to fur,
The dog watching my arm in the hot holt.

Then the birse along his back bristled.
The rabbit made off clean as a whistle
While we two saw someone marvellous,
A lad naked in the bog beside us,
Plunging down till only his head showed
Above water, face at an angle of repose,

Regarding us. He lasted it out.
Enduring hunger, thirst, hardship's butt,
Living by hunting, swift of foot,
Knowing the marsh, taking reed and roots,
Things do not change for him as they do for us:
The dog long dead, I read of tribes in Dio Cassius.

TRANSLATIONS

Flying Geryon

From Canto 17 of Dante's *Inferno,*
(*'Io m'assettai in su quelle spallace . . .'*)

I clambered on the monster's shoulders, and tried
    to speak, but the words wouldn't come
    to voice my wish, 'Oh, hold me tight!'
But he, who at another time had kept
    me from all harm, as soon as I could mount,
    put his arms around me, held me up,
And said, 'Go on now, Geryon, hover
    and wheel about widely, come down gently:
    remember the unusual passenger you have.'
As a small boat casts off from its pier,
    slips gently out, so did the monster shift
    and when it felt that all its girth was clear
There where its breast was, it twisted its tail
    round, stretching and gathering in air,
    it moved off tensed like an eel.
I don't think there was ever such great fear
    even when Phaeton dropped his reins,
    scorching the sky – that mark's still clear;
Not even when poor Icarus in dismay
    felt melted wax upon his back and heard
    his father crying, 'Whoa, not that way!'
As my terror was, when I saw on every side that
    there was air and nothing visible
    or solid save the giddy beast I sat.
It went swimmingly but slowly, slowly
    wheeled and descended; I grew conscious of this
    by the rising wind that rushed me from below.
Already on my right hand side I heard
    a horrid roar of water plunging in the gorge:
    towards that I strained my head and stared.
Now I was more terrified of falling off
    because I could see fires, and hear wailing:
    trembling, I clung on for all I was worth.

For the first time I could see from where we dangled
    our gliding descent swoop among great griefs
    which were approaching me from various angles.
Like a falcon that has hung in the air too long
    without catching sight of any lure or bird,
    till the falconer cries, 'Stoop, come on!'
It comes down tired and slow and makes no sudden
    move, rotating and circling to land far off,
    not beside its master, disdaining him and sullen;
Just so Geryon brought us in to the base,
    the very foot of the perpendicular rock,
    and, being lightened of our bodies,
Vanished like a bolt from taut string's shock.

Virgil Washes the Stains of Hell from Dante's Face with Dew

From Canto 1 of Dante's *Purgatorio*
('*Ei comincio: "Seguisci li miei passi . . ."*')

And he began to say, 'Keep close, my son,
    let's turn round now, for if we go on this way
      the level loses height and slopes down to low ground.'
The hour for matins had begun to flee
    before the dawn's advance, while from this distance off
      I recognised the shimmering of the sea.
We wandered along the lonely plain
    like someone who searches for the road he's lost
      and feels, until he finds it, his efforts are in vain.
When we'd arrived where the dew can resist
    the sun, and because it's always cool there,
      it evaporates slowly, its dampness persists,
my maestro outstretched his hands with gentle care
    spread open on the fresh grass of the place,
      while I, of his purpose well aware,
held up my tear-stained face to him, unbidden;
    he wiped and brought my true colour to light,
      that hue which Hell had hidden.

Charon

From Canto 3 of Dante's *Inferno*
(*E poi che a riguardare oltre mi diedi . . .*)

As I looked further for what this scene could show,
    I saw folk on the bank of a great river;
    so I said, 'Maestro, now will you let me know
who they are, who're ready to cross over,
    and so keen, what instinct urges them on
    as far as I can make out by this light's glimmer.'
And he said to me: 'You'll find out these things soon
    enough, when our footsteps halt
    on the sad shore of Acheron.'
Then, with eyes down, full of shame at my fault,
    afraid that my questioning annoyed him,
    I refrained from speaking till we reached the river-gulch.
But, look, here's an old man who's coming in
    towards us on a wherry, he's whitehaired in hoary mould,
    and calling out: 'Woe to you, souls depraved by sin!
Never hope to see the heavens again, give up your hold!
    I'm coming to take you away to the other shore,
    into the eternal darkness, into heat and cold.
Hoy, you there, living soul, move over more!
    Get away from those who are dead.'
    When he saw I wasn't leaving, but standing as before,
'y another route, by a different harbour,' he said,
    'you'll reach the shore, not here: it's meant
    to be a lighter craft that'll carry you instead.'
My guide said to him, 'Charon, don't take offence.
    This is desired there, where whatever is willed
    can be achieved: ask no more, then.'
The fleecy jowls were dumbstruck, and still
    he clamped his jaws, the helmsman of the livid wave,
    around whose eyes the red flame wheeled.
But those souls, the weary naked wraiths,
    changed colour and began to gnash their teeth
    when they understood Charon's speech was cruel and grave.

They blasted God, cursed their parents with an oath,
    damned all humankind, the place, the time
    and the seed of their conception and their birth.
Then they all huddled together to whine,
    moaning loudly on the evil coast
    which waits for every man who has no God in mind.
Charon the demon, with his eyes of burning coals,
    beckoning to them, gathers in them all,
    and any who linger, he batters with his oar.
Just as in autumn, from the tree leaves fall
    one by one until the branch sees
    there, lying on the ground, are all its spoils;
It's the same when the wicked Adam's seed
    hurl themselves from the shore one after another
    at the signal: for the lure the hawk flies fleet.
So they go off across the black water,
    and before they've disembarked upon the other side
    a fresh crowd on this margin has begun to gather.

On the Highest Cornice

From Canto 25 of Dante's *Purgatorio*
(*'E già venuto all 'ultima tortura . . .'*)

Already we had reached the last twist of the terrace,
    and as we came, turning to our right,
    we had to pay attention to a new menace.
Here the bank fires out sheets of flame
    while air blows upwards from the cornice
    in a blast that beats them back with its aim;
So it was on the exposed edge that we had to go
    in single file, and I feared the fire
    on my left, and on the right, to fall below.
'This is a place' my leader said,
    'where we must keep check on our wandering eyes
    because it would be easy to slip up ahead.'
'*Summae Deus Clementiae*' I heard in the breast
    of the flame, being sung in its hot heart,
    which made me want to look round nevertheless.
I saw spirits moving through the flame;
    so now I looked at them, now watched my steps
    in turn, each look felt a divided claim.
When they'd sung their song through to the end,
    '*Virum non cognosco*', they cried loudly,
    then, softly, started up the hymn again.
As soon as it was finished, they cried 'In the wood
    Diana remained, and chased Helice away
    who'd felt Venus' poison in her blood.'
They tuned their song again, and they gave praise,
    these wives and husbands, faithful as virtue
    and the marriage-vow made chaste.
And I think this way sustains them, it is ample
    for all the time fire burns them and they are annealed.
    It is fitting, with such a remedy and such examples
That the last wound of all be healed.

Dante Talks to the Spirits of the Poets, Guido Guinicelli and Arnaut Daniel

From Canto 26 of Dante's *Purgatorio*
(*'e sanza udire e dir pensoso andai . . .'*)

And I walked without hearing or speaking a word,
    deep in thought, and gazing at him a long while:
    because of the flames, I came no closer than I dared.
Once I had feasted my eyes on him, I offered
    myself, ready to be at his service,
    with the vow that inspires faith in others.
And he said to me, 'What I hear you say
    leaves such a trace in me, so clear
    as Lethe cannot blur or wash away.
But if your oath just now was truly sincere,
    tell me, what's the reason that you show
    when you speak, or look, you hold me dear?'
I answered, 'It's the sweet speech you link
    in verse which, as long as the modern style lasts,
    must make precious its very ink.'
'O brother,' he said, 'I can show you one'
    – and he pointed to a spirit in front –
    'who was a better craftsman of his mother-tongue.
Love-poems or prose romances, he altogether
    surpasses everybody, so let the fools yap
    who think the bard of Limoges is better.
They turn more to what they hear, than to the way
    of truth, and they fix their opinion
    before considering what art or reason have to say.
In the old days, many did so with Guittone,
    the loud-mouths praised him louder until
    truth taught most of them what was phoney.

Now, if you have such high privilege
    that you are allowed to go into the cloister
    where Christ is abbot of the college,
Say for me there, one "Our Father",
    so far as we of this world need your help,
    since it's not in our power to sin further.'
Maybe to make room for others who pressed on
    close to him, he vanished through the flame
    as through deep water, a fish moves and is gone.
I went forward to the soul he'd shown before,
    and said I wished to know his name,
    desiring to write it in a place of honour.
And at once he started to say freely:
    'Yir courtassy sae pleases me, aye whan ye're speirin
    I cuidna, widna lig in derne frae ye:
I am hecht Arnaut, whae greets and gaes singin.
    I think on yon that langsyne wes sae fuilitch,
    an see afore me joy, in joy I'm howpin.
Noo I wis ye, bi yon grace
    bi which ye win awa abune the heuch turn-gree,
    whiles mind on me, wha gets his paiks.'
Then he hid himself in their fiery refinery.

Rock Thrush Alone

From the 19th century Italian of Giacomo Leopardi,
Il Passero Solitario

From your perch on top of the old tower,
Solitary thrush, you sing continually
To the countryside until the day dies
And the melody wanders through this valley.
All around, Spring improvises,
Shines in the brilliant air, runs wild in the fields ;
One look at her melts anybody's mood.
You can hear flocks bleating, herds of cattle lowing,
While the other birds fly a thousand loops,
Skimming and wheeling with speed and grace
In any open space, they celebrate the best of times.
You watch everything, set apart in your own place :
You don't join in, you don't fly,
Their fun and games can pass you by.
You sing, and in this way you spend
The blossomtime of the year and your life's flower.

O no, you are so like me !
Close friends of my youth
Are solace and laughter
Or their companion, longed-for love :
But to those throbs or sighs breathed low
I pay no attention, why, I don't know.
I'd rather avoid their company by far,
Leading the hermit's life, a stranger
To my native place,
Living out this spring.
Day gives way to evening,
It's one they celebrate in our town.
The bell peals in the clear air ;
From one country house to another, echo to echo,
A salvo of rifles resounds, fired to signal the festival.

All dressed up for the holiday
The local youngsters
Leave home to roam the streets :
To see and be seen is the thrill.
Solitary, I wander away
Through the remote outland, keeping aloof
From playful entertainment till some other time.
Meanwhile my gaze roves the field of view
Until the Sun catches my eye
Where behind distant mountains
After a cloudless day
He sinks as he vanishes and seems to say
I'll lose sight of my youth, too.

You, lone little bird, when
You reach the stars' allotted span
Certainly won't regret
The way you spent it : nature prompts
Your every impulse.
Far be it from me to accept
Being pushed to the wall
By hateful old age,
When these eyes can no longer speak to others,
The world is a blur to them, and next day approaches fast
More boring and black than the last.
How will my singular wish appear then ?
What about these years ? how should I see myself again ?
Disconsolate solo, I'll regret the past, I see,
And often turn to look behind me.

Lament for a Blind Harper

From the 17th century Gaelic of Sileas na Ceapaich,
Cumha Lachlainn Daill

Farewell forever to the music of the clarsach
Since death has gripped you, Lachlan:
I'm not fretting for you any more,
I'll never look out to see you again.
I was apprenticed to your music
When I was young, no more than a child;
Although I moved north and away from you,
You used to come visiting my house.

If you never come round here again
A cloud will smother my happiness.
Death hustling you off has caused a mist
Today, like one hanging over a waterfall.
It was you I knew so intimately
And your music I loved so dearly,
There'd be nothing gloomy about our company
Wherever we would sit down together.

When you took up your loved one
And you were tuning her beside me
He's no fool who could appreciate
The variations of your music, my singing of poems.
Sweet your fingers on her set of strings
When I'd ask for the Bishop's Lament,
The Lament for Ranald's Daughter, as well,
Mairi's Lament next, and Gilleasbuig's.

I'll never hear a cadenza again
Or a lament, a salute or a song-tune
But the tears will spring from me
Through deep sorrow that you're not alive.
Though your eyes might have been blind,
You were not blind in one or two ways:
Your lips were not sealed for lovemaking,
You weren't inept when it came to vigour of hand.

I pity your clarsach when I see her being unwrapped,
I grieve at the way it all happened.
I'm sad that you'll never come by again,
And I can never expect to see you.
I ask God to be merciful to you
And to admit you among the angels.
Since your delight on earth was music,
May your soul have music among the saints.

You asked for no more in life
Than you received from noble patrons:
You travelled round with blithe chat and high spirits
For as long as you'd be spending your reward.
What use is it for me to mourn you
After all the maestros who have left us?
And although I loved it in my youth,
Farewell forever to the music of the clarsach.